Ladybird Readers

MOOMIN

The Treasure

Based on the original stories
by Tove Jansson

Picture words

Moomin

Moominmamma

Moominpappa

Snorkmaiden

Little My

fishing rod

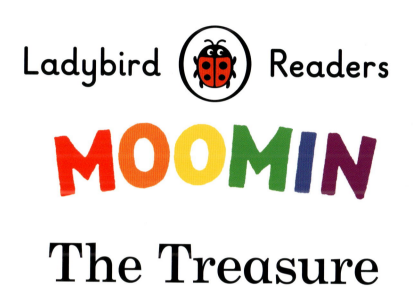

The Treasure

Series Editor: Sorrel Pitts
Text adapted by Mary Taylor
Activities written by Kamini Khanduri

LADYBIRD BOOKS

UK | USA | Canada | Ireland | Australia
India | New Zealand | South Africa

Ladybird Books is part of the Penguin Random House group of companies
whose addresses can be found at global.penguinrandomhouse.com.
www.penguin.co.uk   www.puffin.co.uk   www.ladybird.co.uk

Text adapted from 'Moomin and the Moonlight Adventure'
first published by Puffin Books, 2011
This version published by Ladybird Books Ltd, 2020
001

Printed in China

A CIP catalogue record for this book is available from the British Library

ISBN: 978–0–241–40190–3

All correspondence to:
Ladybird Books
Penguin Random House Children's
80 Strand, London WC2R 0RL

MIX
Paper from
responsible sources
FSC® C018179

top hat

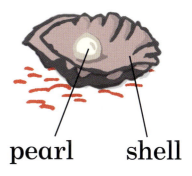

pearl   shell

treasure

asleep

berries

moonlight

When Moomin woke up and saw the sun, he felt happy.

"What a beautiful day!" he said.
"I want to go on a trip.
An exciting trip!"

He went down to the kitchen and said, "Let's go on a boat trip! We can look for treasure!"

"Oh, yes!" thought Snorkmaiden. "What can I wear?"

"Good idea!" said Moominpappa.
"We can go fishing, too."

"And we can take a picnic!"
said Moominmamma.

Moomin liked fishing, but today he couldn't choose a fishing rod.

"Mmm . . . Which one? The red one or the yellow one?" he thought.

Moominpappa couldn't choose
a hat.

"Mmm . . . Which hat for the boat?"
he thought. "The black hat? The
yellow hat for the rain? Or both?
And I must take my top hat,
of course!"

Moominmamma and Little My wanted to take lots of berries with them for the picnic.

"Berries are good to eat," said Moominmamma, "and we can make lots of juice from them, too."

"Good! I love berry juice!" said Little My.

"Mmm! I like berry juice, too!" said Moomin.

"Now, where's Snorkmaiden?" he thought. "Is she ready?"

Snorkmaiden couldn't choose her clothes for the trip.

"Oh dear! What can I wear?" she said. "Can you help me, Moomin?"

"Do you like the blue dress or the pink one?" she asked him.

"They both look nice," said Moomin, "but I like the pink one better."

After many hours, they were all ready and the boat was full.

"Now, let's go and look for treasure!" said Moomin and Snorkmaiden.

Oh dear! It was late!

"There's no sun!" said
Little My, sadly.

"No, there isn't," said Moominpappa,
"but we have the moonlight!"

Then, in the moonlight, they started their trip.

"Let's look for an island!" said Moominpappa.

"Yes!" they all said, happily.

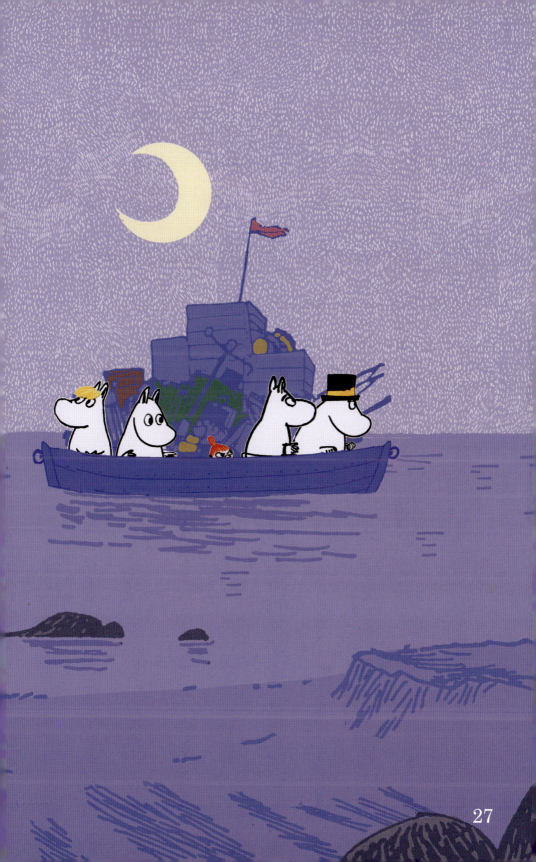

Snorkmaiden was excited. She put her hand into the water.

"There's treasure!" she said. "I can see treasure! Down there!"

"That's not treasure!" said Little My. "It's only the moonlight."

"I think that it's treasure!" said Moomin.

Then, Moomin jumped into the water.

He swam down and down and down . . .

At the bottom, he saw a beautiful pearl inside a shell!

Snorkmaiden, Little My, Moominmamma, and Moominpappa all looked into the water, but they couldn't see Moomin.

"Oh dear," said Snorkmaiden. "Is he all right?"

Then, Moomin swam back to the boat.

"Oh, Moomin!" said Snorkmaiden, happily.

"It WAS treasure!" said Moomin. "Look!"

He showed Snorkmaiden the beautiful shell. The pearl inside it was the same color as the moon.

"It's beautiful!" said Snorkmaiden.

"It's for you!" said Moomin.

After a few minutes, Moominpappa
saw something.

"I can see an island!" he said.

"Good!" said Moominmamma.
"Let's have our picnic there."

They made a nice fire and enjoyed their picnic in the moonlight.

Moominpappa told them stories about the sea.

They talked most about Moomin
and the pearl.

Then, they all felt very tired.

Snorkmaiden put her head next to Moomin's head.

"Thank you, Moomin!" she said.
"Thank you for my treasure.
It's beautiful!"

Moomin was very, very happy!

"Tomorrow, I can find you more treasure," he said.

Snorkmaiden didn't hear him—she was asleep!

Activities

The key below describes the skills practiced in each activity.

Spelling and writing

Reading

Speaking

Critical thinking

Preparation for the Cambridge Young Learners exams

1 **Match the words to the pictures.**

1 Moomin

2 Moominmamma

3 Moominpappa

4 Snorkmaiden

5 Little My

a

b

c

d

e

2 Circle the correct words.

When Moomin woke up and saw the sun, he felt happy.

"What a beautiful day!" he said. "I want to go on a trip. An exciting trip!"

6

1 When Moomin woke up, he saw

  a the moon.   **b** the sun.

2 He felt

  a happy.   **b** hungry.

3 It was a beautiful

  a day.   **b** dress.

4 Moomin wanted to go on a

  a bed.   **b** trip.

3 **Look and read. Put a** ✓ **or a** ✗ **in the boxes.**

1  This is Moomin. ✓

2 This is a red fishing rod. ☐

3  This is a yellow hat. ☐

4  This is a top hat. ☐

5  This is Moominpappa. ☐

4 **Look and read. Write the answers as complete sentences.**

Moominmamma and Little My wanted to take lots of berries with them for the picnic.

"Berries are good to eat," said Moominmamma, "and we can make lots of juice from them, too."

"Good! I love berry juice!" said Little My.

14   15

1 What did Moominmamma want to take for the picnic?

She wanted berries.

2 What could they make from berries?

....

3 Who loved berry juice?

....

5 **Write the correct sentences.**

1 (couldn't) (Snorkmaiden) (her) (clothes) (choose) (.)

Snorkmaiden couldn't
choose her clothes.

2 (can) (wear) (I) ("What) (?")

....

3 (help) (you) (me,) (Moomin) ("Can) (?")

....

4 (blue) (the) (dress) (like) (you) ("Do) (?")

....

....

6 **Read the story. Choose the correct words and write them next to 1—4.**

1	never	all	always
2	let's	let	lets
3	sad	sadder	sadly
4	isnt	hasn't	isn't

After many hours, they were [1] _____all_____

ready and the boat was full.

"Now, [2] _____ go and look for

treasure!" said Moomin and Snorkmaiden.

"There's no sun!" said Little My,

[3] _____. "No, there [4] _____,"

said Moominpappa.

7 **Look and read. Write *true* or *false*.**

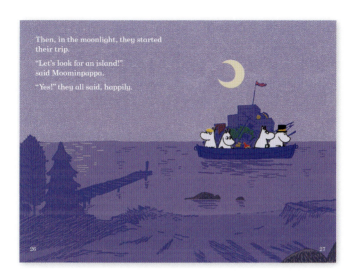

Then, in the moonlight, they started their trip.

"Let's look for an island!" said Moominpappa.

"Yes!" they all said, happily.

1 It was morning.　　　　　false

2 Moominpappa wore
a top hat.

3 There were three people in
the boat.

4 They wanted to find berries.

5 There was moonlight.

8 **Match the two parts of the sentences. Then, write them on the lines.** 📖 ✏️

1 Then, in the moonlight,

2 "Let's look for an island!"

3 "Yes!" they

a said Moominpappa.

b all said, happily.

c they started their trip.

1 Then, in the moonlight, they started their trip.

2 ....

....

3 ....

....

9 **Look at the letters. Write the words.**

t e x d i c e

1 Snorkmaiden was ..excited...

t r e w a

2 She put her hand into the

....

r a s t e r u e

3 "I can see ....!" she said.

g l o o m h i n t

4 "It's only the ....," said Little My.

k n i t h

5 "I .... that it's treasure!" said Moomin.

55

10 Find the words.

agbr(pearl)sepmdwaterthikjumpedwhceopshelljafidownbmurewswamcojr

pearl

water

swam

down

jumped

shell

11 **Write the correct form of the verbs.** 📖 ✏️

They all _____looked_____ **(look)** into the water, but they _____ **(can't)** see Moomin.

"Oh dear," said Snorkmaiden, "_____ **(be)** he all right?"

Then, Moomin _____ **(swim)** back to the boat.

"Oh, Moomin!" _____ **(say)** Snorkmaiden, happily.

12 **Write the missing letters.**

| u r e   e a r   h i n   o o n   e l l |

1 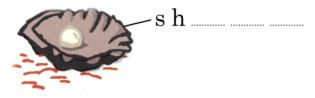 t r e a s ....u....r.... e

2  s h ....

3  m ....

4 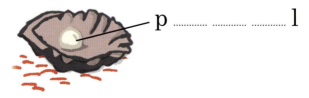 f i s .... g
r o d

5 p l

13 Read the text. Choose the correct words and write them next to 1—5.

> made   felt   talked   told   enjoyed

They [1] _made_ a nice fire and [2] _____ their picnic in the moonlight. Moominpappa [3] _____ them stories about the sea. They [4] _____ most about Moomin and the pearl. Then, they all [5] _____ very tired.

14 **Ask and answer the questions with a friend.** 💬 ❓

They made a nice fire and enjoyed their picnic in the moonlight.

Moominpappa told them stories about the sea.

They talked most about Moomin and the pearl.

Then, they all felt very tired.

1 *What did they enjoy?*

They enjoyed a picnic.

2 What did Moominpappa tell them?

3 What did they talk most about?

4 Why did they make a fire, do you think?

15 **Read the questions. Write answers using the words in the box.**

> next to   happy   asleep   treasure

1 Where did Snorkmaiden put her head?

<u>She put her head next to</u>
<u>Moomin's head.</u>

2 What did Moomin feel?

....

....

3 What did Moomin say?

....

....

4 Why didn't Snorkmaiden hear him?

....

....

16 **Talk about the two pictures with a friend. How are they different?**

In picture a, Moomin is on his bed. In picture b, Moomin and Snorkmaiden are on a beach.

17 **Order the story. Write 1—5.**

.... Moomin swam down and down.
He found a beautiful pearl inside
a shell. It was treasure!

.... They started their trip in the
moonlight. Snorkmaiden put her
hand in the water. Then, Moomin
jumped into the water.

....1.... Moomin wanted to go on a boat trip
to look for treasure. He liked fishing,
but he couldn't choose a fishing rod.

.... They made a fire and enjoyed
their picnic. They talked and told
stories. Then, they all felt very
tired. Snorkmaiden was asleep!

.... Moominmamma and Little My
wanted to take berries for a picnic.

Ladybird Readers

Visit www.ladybirdeducation.co.uk
for more FREE Ladybird Readers resources

- ✓ Digital edition of every title*
- ✓ Audio tracks (US/UK)
- ✓ Answer keys
- ✓ Lesson plans

- ✓ Role-plays
- ✓ Classroom display material
- ✓ Flashcards
- ✓ User guides

Register and sign up to the newsletter to receive your FREE classroom resource pack!

*Ladybird Readers series only. Not applicable to *Peppa Pig* books.
Digital versions of Ladybird Readers books available once book has been purchased.